Christmas break is starting and the family is getting ready for a new journey. This time they are traveling to Chile, a long narrow country in South America situated between the Pacific Ocean and the Andes mountain range.

Chile has more than 100 active volcanoes. On this trip George, who is an environmental scientist, will be recording changes to the regional flora that have occurred as a result of the eruption of the Puyehue-Cordón Caulle volcano in 2011. During this project, the family will visit many interesting places.

They board a plane in Dallas, Texas and 10 hours later land in Santiago, the capital of Chile.

"Mom, I want to go to the main square of the city!" says Aya impatiently. "And I want to climb the hill I read about in the tourist book," adds Nick.

Aya gets her wish when their first stop is the Plaza de Armas. The kids run around the fountain and explore the historic part of the capital.

At a local food stand they buy MOTE CON HUESILLO and the children try their first traditional Chilean food, husked wheat soaked in a kind of peachy nectar.

In the evening, Nick gets his wish. They climb the rocky stairs of Santa Lucia Hill and from its top they observe the skyline of the city.

"That very tall building you see," Kate tells them, "is called Gran Torre Santiago; in English, Great Santiago Tower. It has 62 floors and is 300 meters (984 feet) high."

From the capital the family goes to Valparaiso, a colorful city with seaside cliffs, lots of hills and long staircases.

"Look at all these drawings on the walls of the buildings!" Nick exclaims, his eyes wide with wonder.

"This city is known for its street art and murals. Any artist is allowed to draw or paint on these walls," George explains.

From Valparaiso they drive to San Pedro de Atacama, a road trip that takes a couple of days. On the way, they spend a day at the beach on a beautiful bay called Bahia Inglesa.

"Aya, come with me! I want you to see the colorful seaweed I found!" Nick calls out to his sister.

The two spend hours playing on the beach, climbing unique rock formations, collecting shells, and finding various sea creatures.

The family finally reaches the small town of San Pedro de Atacama in the desert, which becomes their home for a few days.

Nick grabs his father's attention, shouting, "Is that a volcano? It has something coming out of its top!"

"Yes. Some of the volcanoes spit gases off and on all day every day, like this one that you've noticed. Look, it has stopped now, but it will start again. Just observe," suggests George to his son.

"Today we are going to visit a Moon Valley and see various geologic formations," says Kate.
"Why is it called a Moon Valley?" asks Aya.
"Moon Valley resembles the landscape of the Moon. It is a very unique sight!"

"And what about seeing geysers? I remember geysers in Kamchatka and dad told us that we would see them in Chile too," pleads Aya.

"Yes dear, we will visit El Tatio geyser tomorrow. It is the largest field of geysers in the southern hemisphere. We will reach very high mountains to see it," responds her mother.

On the last day of the Atacama adventure they go to the hidden lagoons of Baltinache.

"These are seven turquoise colored miniature lakes filled with saline water. You can see that each one is unique in its shape and size, and the formation of its salt crystals. Kids, you can observe this natural beauty, but please stay on the marked trail and respect the rules," instructs George.

"Ok Dad!" Nick and Aya gladly agree while staring at crystalline forms of salt and blue water surrounded by the brown landscape of the Atacama Desert.

When they leave Atacama, they take a local flight from Calama to Valdivia, a city founded in the year of 1552.

The family visits a local market on the bank of the river.
"Mom, look at all this seafood sold here!" Nick is smiling. "And
look at the sea lions sitting on the shore!"
"Why are they here?" asks Aya.
"It seems like they are waiting for seafood leftovers they get
from the market vendors," suggests Kate.

The kids get hungry and each eat a
COMPLETO, a type of Chilean
hotdog served with chopped
tomatoes, mayonnaise, mashed
avocado and sauerkraut.

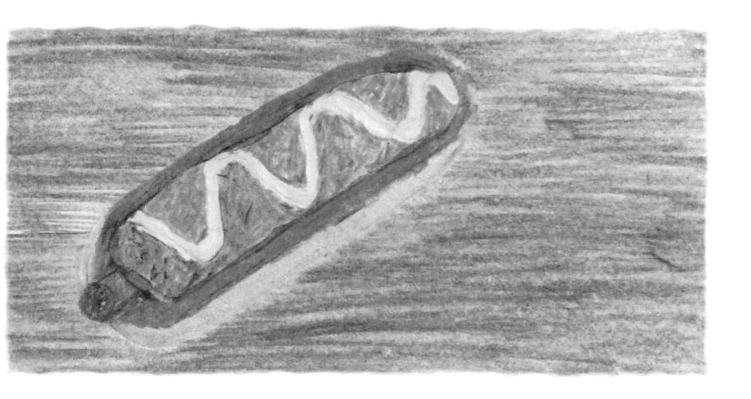

After they eat, George is ready to move on.

"Are you all ready to drive for a little while and see a volcano that erupted in 2011 and covered a large area with ash? The eruption was so strong that the ash reached Argentina and its neighboring country Uruguay."

"If it covered that large an area with ash, what happened to the flowers and insects?" asks Aya.

"Very good question!" George responds. "Major eruptions cause a lot of damage. That one increased the temperature of the nearby river which killed millions of fish. Heat and ash killed plants and trees. And with no grass to eat, many animals such as deer, sheep and cows were harmed, and many died."

"That sounds really bad, Dad," Nick frowns.
"Yes, it was a serious event with very long lasting consequences. Everything on our planet is connected," the father reminds his kids.

When they reach the area of Puyehue-Cordón Caulle Volcano George takes samples of plants and stores them in special containers for later studies.

From the volcano they drive to Pucon, an area known for another volcano and multiple hot springs. They spend a day swimming in hot and warm pools of water which bubbles to the surface from deep within the Earth's crust. They especially like a place called El Rincón, which has a view of a waterfall.

From TERMAS, which is the Spanish word for hot springs, the family continues their drive south on the Carretera Austral, the famous road in Chile that winds through very beautiful countryside with mountains, streams, flower fields and waterfalls.

"Dad, you said that this road will end when we reach a bay and there is no bridge. How are we going to get across?" asks Nick.

"A ferry will take us across!" responds George.

"Wow! I have never been on a ferry before. Our car is inside a boat. This is so exciting!" shouts Aya.

"Dad, remember I caught a Brook Trout in Argentine Patagonia? Aren't we in Chilean Patagonia now? I wonder what we will catch here?" asks Nick.

The next day they arrive at the Rio Cisnes. George and Nick enjoy an afternoon of fly fishing, and Nick catches his first ever King Salmon, a huge fish!

"Mom, I see this flower growing all over different trees and bushes! What is it called?" asks Aya.

"It is called Copihue and it is the national flower of Chile. Doesn't it resemble a little bell?!" suggests Kate to her daughter.

Soon the travellers reach Torres del Paine National Park.

"The water is so turquoise here, very similar to the lagoons in Atacama. Is it salty too?" asks Nick.

"No, this is fresh water that melted from the glacier. Do you want to take a boat and get closer to it?" asks George.

"This glacier is similar to Perito Moreno Glacier in Argentina. I remember we visited it last year," recalls Aya.

For dinner they go to a restaurant inside the park and all try hot CAZUELA, a traditional Chilean dish cooked with meat, potatoes and pumpkin.

Before leaving the National Park, Nick and Aya and their parents take a long hike to see the mountain towers of Torres del Paine that surround a beautiful lake high in the Andes.

MAGDALENA ISLAND
PUNTA ARENAS
STRAIT OF MAGELLAN
TIERRA DEL FUEGO

Their final destination in Chilean Patagonia is an island called Magdalena which is located in the Strait of Magellan. They take a boat from Punta Arenas to the island and stay on it all day watching penguins in their natural habitat.

"These are Magellanic Penguins!" says Nick to his sister.

"Look mommy, that penguin is sitting on its egg! She will have babies soon! Aww, I want to hold a baby penguin!" exclaims Aya.

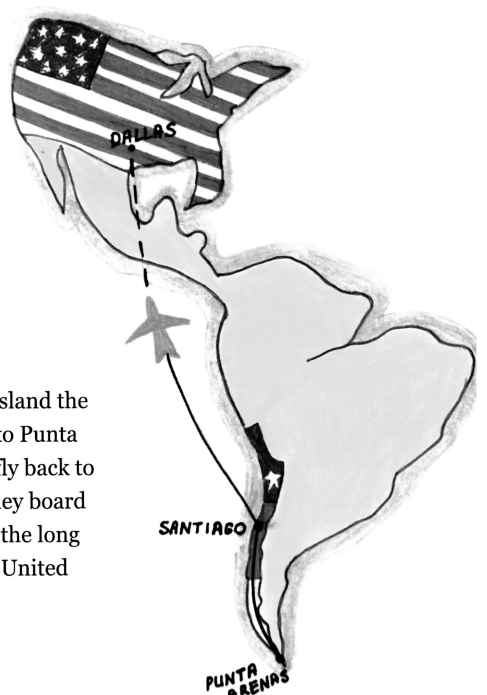

From Magdalena Island the family goes back to Punta Arenas. They then fly back to Santiago, where they board another plane for the long trip home to the United States.

This book is dedicated to my daughter Aya who started traveling the world when she was 6 weeks old, and to my husband Justin who makes these travels possible.

Made in United States
Orlando, FL
10 March 2022

15638837R10022